BUCKINGHAM PALACE

BUCKINGHAM PALACE

THE PALACE AND ITS ROYAL RESIDENTS IN PHOTOGRAPHS

MICHAEL HALL

a Salamander book

Published by Salamander Books Limited
LONDON

A Salamander Book

Distributed by Random House Value Publishing, Inc.
40 Engelhard Avenue
Avenel, New Jersey 07001

A CIP catalog record for this book is available from the Library of Congress.

© Salamander Books Ltd 1995

ISBN: 0-517-12158-1

All correspondence concerning the content of this book should be addressed to Salamander Books Ltd., 129-137 York Way, London N7 9LG, England.

CREDITS:

Editor: Krystyna Zukowksa
Designer: John Heritage
Typesetting: SX Composing Ltd, England
Color reproduction: P & W Graphics PTE Ltd, Singapore

Printed in Belgium

9 8 7 6 5 4 3 2 1

Prelim captions: Front cover: Queen Elizabeth photographed by Cecil Beaton in the grounds of Buckingham Palace; Back cover: The coronation procession of Queen Elizabeth II; Front and back endpapers: The garden house at Buckingham Palace; page 1: The wedding of the Prince and Princess of Wales; page 2: Birthday portrait of the Queen by Cecil Beaton; page 4: Guests arriving at Buckingham Palace for a garden party; page 5: The wedding of Princess Elizabeth and the Duke of Edinburgh.

PICTURE CREDITS

The Publishers would like to thank the photo agencies and photographers who have supplied photographs for this book. The photographs are credited by page number and position on the page as follows: (T) Top; (B) Bottom, etc.

The Publishers have endeavored to ensure that all the photographs in this book are correctly credited. Should any illustration in this book be incorrectly attributed, the Publishers apologize.

Front cover: Cecil Beaton/Camera Press, London; **Back cover:** Hulton Deutsch; **Front and back endpapers:** National Monuments Record; **1:** Hulton Deutsch; **2:** Cecil Beaton/Camera Press, London; **4:** Hulton Deutsch; **5:** Hulton Deutsch; **6:** National Portrait Gallery, London (T); Museum of London (B); **7:** British Architectural Library, RIBA, London; **8:** National Monuments Record (T); Popperfoto (B); **9:** Camera Press, London; **10:** Country Life Picture Library (T); Country Life Picture Library (B); **11:** Country Life Picture Library (T); Country Life Picture Library (B); **12:** Camera Press, London (T); National Monuments Record (B); **13:** Camera Press, London; **14:** Camera Press, London; **15:** Camera Press, London (T); Hulton Deutsch (B); **16:** Popperfoto (T); Popperfoto (B); **17:** Popperfoto; **18:** Popperfoto; **19:** Camera Press, London; **20:** Hulton Deutsch (T); Hulton Deutsch (B); **21:** Hulton Deutsch; **22:** Country Life Picture Library (T); Camera Press, London (B); **23:** Greater London Photographic Library; **24:** Country Life Picture Library (T); Country Life Picture Library (B); **25:** Country Life Picture Library; **26:** Country Life Picture Library; **27:** Country Life Picture Library (T); Country Life Picture Library (B); **28:** Mr Grinell, National Monuments Record; **29:** Camera Press, London: **30:** Hulton Deutsch (T); Hulton Deutsch (B); **31:** Camera Press, London; **32:** Hulton Deutsch (T); Hulton Deutsch (B); **33:** Hulton Deutsch (T); Hulton Deutsch (B); **34:** Dorothy Wilding/Camera Press, London (T); Hulton Deutsch (B); **35:** BARON/Camera Press, London; **36:** BARON/Camera Press, London; **37:** Dorothy Wilding/Camera Press, London (T); Dorothy Wilding/Camera Press, London (B); **38:** Cecil Beaton/Camera Press, London; **39:** Cecil Beaton/Camera Press, London (L); Cecil Beaton/Camera Press, London (R); **40:** Hulton Deutsch (T); Hulton Deutsch (B); **41:** National Monuments Record; **42:** Hulton Deutsch (T); Camera Press, London (B); **43:** Camera Press, London; **44:** Camera Press, London (T); Camera Press, London (B); **45:** Cecil Beaton/Camera Press, London; **46:** Cecil Beaton/Camera Press, London (T); Camera Press, London (B); **47:** Cecil Beaton/Camera Press, London; **48:** Hulton Deutsch (T); Hulton Deutsch (B); **49:** Hulton Deutsch; **50:** Cecil Beaton/Camera Press, London (T); Camera Press, London (B); **51:** Cecil Beaton/Camera Press, London; **52:** Patrick Lichfield/Camera Press, London (T); Norman Parkinson/Camera Press, London (B); **53:** Camera Press, London (T); Camera Press, London (B); **54:** Camera Press, London (T); Camera Press, London (B); **55:** Camera Press, London (T); Camera Press, London (B); **56:** Colour Library International (T); Camera Press, London (B); **57:** Srdja Djukanovic/Camera Press, London (T); Camera Press, London (B); **58:** Range/Bettmann/UPI (T); Range/Bettmann/UPI (B); **59:** Range/Bettmann/UPI (T); Range/Bettmann/UPI (B); **60:** Patrick Lichfield/Camera Press, London (T); Patrick Lichfield/Camera Press, London (B); **61:** Patrick Lichfield/Camera Press, London (T); Hulton Deutsch (B); **62:** Patrick Lichfield/Camera Press, London; **63:** Patrick Lichfield/Camera Press, London (T); Glenn Harvey/Camera Press, London (B); **64:** B. Howarth-Loomes/National Monuments Record.

CONTENTS

INTRODUCTION

Daily life for the royal family in London takes place against the backdrop of one of the most famous buildings in the world, yet until 1993, when it opened its doors to the public for the first time, Buckingham Palace was for most people a mysterious building. Passers-by see only the imperial dignity of the façade given to it shortly before the First World War. However, this familiar pedimented front, together with the balcony on which the royal family makes public appearances, usually at weddings or jubilees, was the last part to be built. That façade hides many layers of history: for all the self-confidence with which Buckingham Palace now stares down the Mall, its story is one of compromise, all too often accompanied by muddle and scandal.

The first monarch to be involved with the site of the palace was James I. In 1609 he bought some land just to the north of St James's Park where he

Above: George IV, the monarch responsible for the creation of Buckingham Palace. His work there began in 1825 but was still not completed when he died in 1830, having overspent dramatically.

laid out a silkworm farm, in an unsuccessful attempt to establish an English silk-weaving industry. In the 1630s the site became a public pleasure ground, part of which was let to George Goring, the Earl of Norwich, so that he could extend the garden of his mansion, Goring House, which was next door. Soon after 1674 this house, by then owned by the Earl of Arlington was entirely rebuilt. It passed by descent to the third Earl of Mulgrave, who in 1702 demolished it and built an entirely new house on a slightly different site. Christened "Buckingham House" in honor of the dukedom granted to Lord Mulgrave in 1703, this house is the kernel of the present palace, to which it has given its name.

In 1742 the house was inherited by the Duke of Buckingham's illegitimate son, Sir Charles Sheffield, who soon made the unwelcome discovery that a substantial part had been built

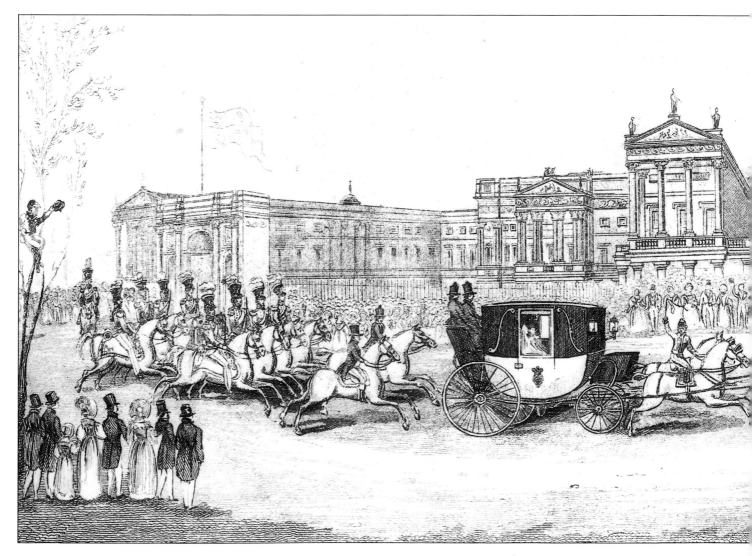

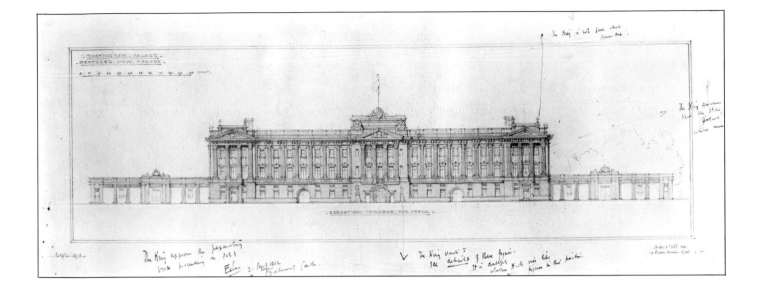

Below: Queen Victoria with Prince Albert, her new husband, leave Buckingham Palace after their official wedding celebrations. This print shows the main front of the palace in the early 1830s.

Above: Aston Webb's 1912 design for the remodeling of the palace's Victorian façade. George V's comments can be observed: for example (on the urns), "The King is not sure what these are".

on Crown land, held to a 99-year lease granted in 1672. He decided to cut his losses and in 1762 sold Buckingham House to the young George III for £28,000. The official reason for the purchase was the need to provide a dower house for Queen Charlotte, whom the King had married the previous year, but from the beginning it was intended to serve as the monarch's principal private London home. As official Court functions continued to be held at St James's Palace, there was no immediate need to make any dramatic changes to the house. However, the King's growing family eventually led to several large extensions, mostly carried out by the architect William Chambers.

The decision to convert Buckingham Palace from a private residence to a public palace was taken by George III and Queen Charlotte's eldest son, George, the Prince Regent, who became George IV in 1820.

George IV was an outstanding connoisseur and collector who was prepared to pay high prices to achieve work of the highest quality. Needless to say, this was not a trait which endeared him to a parsimonious Government, which – with good reason – suspected that he was

capable of reckless extravagance. Yet the King was determined to create an architectural symbol of Britain's new role as a world power and the conqueror of Napoleon.

By choosing John Nash as his architect, George IV was assured of an architect capable of realizing this ideal with flair, as he knew from the work Nash had carried out for him at the Brighton Pavilion, the King's wonderfully eccentric seaside home. However, Nash was not noted for financial discipline and he was faced with a 62 year old patron when work began who was impatient to see the building finished. From the beginning, their collaboration had the makings of an artistic triumph but a financial disaster: "It was impossible to conform to the Estimates", wrote Nash in 1831, recalling his relationship with his royal master: "Whenever I saw him, it generally happened that he ordered some alteration." Costs soon spiraled out of control.

Nash finally met his nemesis after George IV's death in June 1830, when it was revealed that he had spent £35,000 more than his revised estimates, and there was still a great deal of work to be done. The Treasury withdrew the architect's commission, dismissed him from his official appointments and put a stop to the work. Nash had to answer for himself before a Parliamentary Select Committee, and although he was cleared of charges of corruption and poor workmanship, he was found guilty of "inexcusable irregularity

and great negligence". The completion of the building was put in the hands of Edward Blore, a rather dull architect. Blore made some substantial changes to the exterior of the Palace, and completed Nash's opulently refined state rooms. The final estimate, which Blore naturally respected, was £613,260, approximately two-and-a-half times as much as Nash had originally predicted.

Above: This Edwardian photograph shows the range added to the front of the palace in 1855. Designed by Edward Blore, it converted Nash's open court into a closed quadrangle. Its design drew much criticism, especially when the stonework began to crumble. The new façade designed by Webb (below), built in 1913, is a much more satisfactory public face for the palace.

The one person who did not seem to be pleased that work was coming to an end was the palace's intended occupant, King William IV. He was quite happy with his modest domestic life in Clarence House and hated the idea of having to move into an extravagant new house built by his spendthrift brother and although Buckingham Palace was ready for occupation in 1834, it was another three years before it would receive its first royal resident.

This did not stop public inspection of the building, which was surprisingly accompanied by much hostile criticism. "As for our Buckingham Palace", wrote Thomas Creevey, "never was there such a specimen of wicked, vulgar profusion. It has cost a million of money, and there is not a fault that has not been committed in it... Raspberry-coloured pillars without end that turn you quite sick to look at". Others, however, appreciated those qualities of Nash's interiors which are most likely to impress visitors today: the near-Baroque effect of the plasterwork ceilings, for example, or the importance of sculpture, not only in friezes and bas-reliefs but also in chimneypieces and door-cases of marble.

This richness was designed to set off the King's splendid collections of furniture and paintings, which are still the chief treasures of the palace. Even George IV's sternest critics could not deny that he had a superb eye for artistic quality. In Nash he had an architect capable of living up to his standards, and it is remarkable that together they were capable of creating rooms of this quality at great speed. What remains most memorable is the complexity of the decorative effects, for Nash effortlessly synthesised the skills of his craftsmen – metalworkers, sculptors, plasterworkers, parquet makers, upholsterers and manufacturers of scagliola and etched and mirror glass – into a spectacular unity.

Nash's brilliantly theatrical staircase ascends in two directions to the principal floor. The double flight leads northwards into the principal suite of ceremonial rooms, the Guard Room, Green Drawing Room and Throne Room. A single flight leads into an even more magnificent suite of three drawing rooms on the garden front: the White Drawing Room, the Music Room, which has a great bow window and a notable marquetry floor, and the Blue Drawing Room. The two suites are linked by a long, top-lit picture gallery.

These splendid rooms thrilled the palace's first royal occupant, the 18-year-old Princess Victoria, who succeeded to the throne in June 1837 and held her first ball at Buckingham Palace the following May. Victoria enjoyed herself enormously that evening: "I had not danced for so long and was so glad to do so again", although some of the crustier members of court were a little shocked by her youthful refusal to stand on ceremony.

Yet after her marriage to Prince Albert of Saxe-Coburg-Gotha in 1840, and the rapid appearance of numerous children, Queen Victoria soon came to realize that a palace designed for a childless, widower King was too small for her needs. In 1845 a new extension, partly financed by the sale of the Brighton Pavilion, was at last begun, to the designs of Blore. Unfortunately, but predictably, this consisted of an entire new range on the east side of the palace, so converting Nash's open courtyard facing on to the Mall into a closed quadrangle. Nobody much liked Blore's rather fussy design, and so it was perhaps a blessing in disguise that the new range was built of Caen stone, which is very vulnerable to acid rain. Thanks to London's polluted air, the stonework was discernibly crumbling by 1853, and was later painted to hide the scars. Rather more successful was

Below: Buckingham Palace from the air. The Mall and the Queen Victoria Memorial are at the top of the photograph, the gardens and the state apartments at the bottom. The large extension on the right houses the ballroom, built in 1855.

the second great extension, at the south-west corner of the palace, which contained a large ballroom and a supper room, designed by James Pennethorne. He was forestalled in other proposed changes by the sudden death of Prince Albert in December 1861.

Once the Queen had emerged from her deepest mourning, she continued to use Buckingham Palace for the customary round of court ceremonies, but was not prepared to brook any changes. Even Prince Albert's rooms were maintained exactly as he had left them. Not surprisingly, the accession of the Queen's eldest son as Edward VII in 1901 was followed by a wholesale re-

Left: The White Drawing Room. This, and the photographs on the following pages are part of the finest photographic record ever made of the palace's state rooms.

Below: The Grand Staircase. Its magnificent balustrade was made by Samuel Parker in 1828-30.

furbishment and redecoration of the palace, which he once called "the sepulchre". Out went the rich and ornate Victorian decoration, to be replaced by simple white and gold schemes in a French manner. The most radical change followed the accession of George V in 1910, when it was decided to create a new façade for the building, using surplus money raised for the Queen Victoria Memorial in front of the palace. The designer of the memorial, Aston Webb, was responsible for the new façade, which is no more than a skin on Blore's building. It was erected in the astonishingly short period of thirteen weeks in the summer of 1913. George V asked for a significant change to the design before building began: he wanted the balcony to project further, because it was to be "used from time to time on occasions when the King and other members of the Royal Family wish to show themselves to the people". The transformation of a once modest private house into the backdrop for the very public workings of a modern monarchy was complete.

Above: The Picture Gallery, which was remodeled in 1914 for George V. Its original appearance is shown in the photograph on pages 16-17. Many of the greatest paintings in the Royal Collection are hung there.

Below: The Throne Room, which is decorated with dramatic plasterwork. The genii holding garlands are especially notable; above them is a frieze, designed by Thomas Stothard, which depicts the Wars of the Roses.

THE VICTORIAN ERA

Right: Queen Victoria in 1897, as she is best remembered today: Queen Empress and regal matriarch, loyally tending the memory of her departed husband and unwilling to brook changes at Buckingham Palace or any of her other homes.

Below: The garden front of Buckingham Palace in 1900. The sentry stands in front of steps which lead up to the conservatory. A pavilion at the end of the palace was also designed as a conservatory, but later was converted into the chapel.

Above: Queen Victoria in 1883, a
year after her Golden Jubilee, the
event which persuaded her to take a
more active part in public life. For
once the somber black clothes have
been replaced by more opulent ones.

Left: Prince Albert, Queen Victoria's beloved husband, who reorganized the running of the palace on more efficient lines and oversaw many alterations and additions to the building.

Right: Queen Victoria with her eldest son, later Edward VII, and his Danish wife, Alexandra. When Edward succeeded to the throne in 1901, he set about redecorating Buckingham Palace, creating white and gold French-inspired schemes which have mostly survived to the present day.

Below: This photograph of Edward VII's study provides a rare glimpse into his private apartments.

Three interiors of Buckingham Palace in the 19th century. The ballroom (above) was added in 1855, as Queen Victoria decided that Nash's state rooms were too cramped. The photograph shows the rich decoration commissioned by Prince Albert which was painted out by Edward VII.

Right: The Picture Gallery, as it appeared before remodeling in 1914. Note Nash's quirky ceiling, which included little glazed domes separated by pendants.

Below: The Throne Room, with a single throne for Queen Victoria.

Right: A glimpse into Queen Victoria's daily life in the palace: dressed in her characteristic black, she is being read to by a companion in the palace gardens.

Below: The chapel in the 19th century, decorated for a special occasion. Converted from a conservatory in 1842-43, shortly after Queen Victoria's marriage, it was destroyed by a German bomb in September 1940. After World War II the shell was converted into a public gallery where temporary exhibitions of works from the Royal Collection are held.

Below: Edward VII is the only monarch to have died at Buckingham Palace, just as he was the first to have been born there. Crowds were photographed outside the palace, anxiously awaiting news of his health. Almost the last words he uttered, shortly before his death on May 6, 1910, were to acknowledge with pleasure the news that his horse, "Witch of the Air", had won the 4.15 race at Kempton Park. Before the funeral his coffin lay in state in the Throne Room at Buckingham Palace (left).

Right: An impressive array of the foreign monarchs who attended the funeral were photographed at the palace with the new king, George V. Standing, left to right, are: Haakon VII of Norway, Ferdinand I of Bulgaria, Alanoel II of Portugal, Kaiser Wilhelm II of Germany, Gustav V of Sweden and Albert I of Belgium. Seated at the front, from left to right, are: Alphonso XIII of Spain, George V and Frederick VIII of Denmark.

Left: The Mall and the Queen Victoria Memorial from the balcony of Buckingham Palace. This is the view the royal family enjoy when they wave to the crowds below.

Above: George V's reign saw the establishment in the public mind of the British monarchy as an ideal family as well as a royal household. For the first time, such occasions as weddings, previously celebrated in private, became part of the round of public ceremonies at Buckingham Palace. Major events were marked by the royal family's appearance on the balcony of the palace's new façade, shown above under construction in the summer of 1913.

The photograph on the left celebrates a royal event of 1926: the baptism of Princess Elizabeth. Ten years later, the abdication of her uncle, Edward VIII, would unexpectedly make her the heir to the throne. She is being held by her mother, the Duchess of York (the future Queen Elizabeth, the Queen Mother); her father, the Duke of York, the future George VI, stands behind his wife to the right, between his father, George V, and father-in-law, the Earl of Strathmore. Queen Mary sits on the left of the Duchess, the Countess of Strathmore and Princess Mary, the Princess Royal (George V and Queen Mary's only daughter) to her right.

Right: In 1936 the *Country Life* photographer A. E. Henson made a record of the private rooms at Buckingham Palace for Queen Mary. Henson's pictures form a record of the taste of one of the first members of the royal family to have an appreciation of the palace's history and treasures. Her best-known contribution to the interiors was the decoration of the central rooms on the east front, with Regency chinoiserie furnishings from Brighton Pavilion that had been in storage since the 1850s.

Above: The Queen's bedroom was hung with portraits of her children. The overall effect of the room was one of light and airiness.

Below: When she moved in, in 1910, her predecessor, Queen Alexandra, was alarmed to hear of the changes being made to rooms that Queen Mary found intolerably over-furnished: "*Our* dear old rooms", she wrote to Queen Mary, "I shall indeed be very curious and anxious to see them & how you have arranged it all."

The ballroom at Buckingham Palace: This 1930 photograph (left) shows two thrones, for George V and Queen Mary, on the dais. Behind them is a gold-embroidered canopy adapted from the imperial *shamiana* under which George V and Queen Mary had sat in 1911 during the Delhi Durbar (the ceremonial gathering of their Indian subjects to pay homage). The thrones on the right, embroidered with the ciphers of George V and Queen Mary, were photographed in the throne room.

Below: Another view of Queen Mary's bedroom: the portraits are of her two eldest sons, the Prince of Wales (later Edward VIII) and the Duke of York (later George VI).

Right: George V and Queen Mary leave Buckingham Palace on June 22, 1911, on the way to the coronation. "Magnificent reception both going and coming back", wrote Queen Mary in her diary that evening, "There were hundreds and thousands of people". The Royal State Coach circles the Victoria Memorial, the monument to his grandmother which George V had recently unveiled.

Below: Two years later, work began on the refacing of the palace's main façade, as shown on pages 7-8. One of the most splendid details of that work was the intricate metalwork of the new forecourt gates, executed by the Bromsgrove Guild: the cherubs gamboling around the locks are especially delightful.

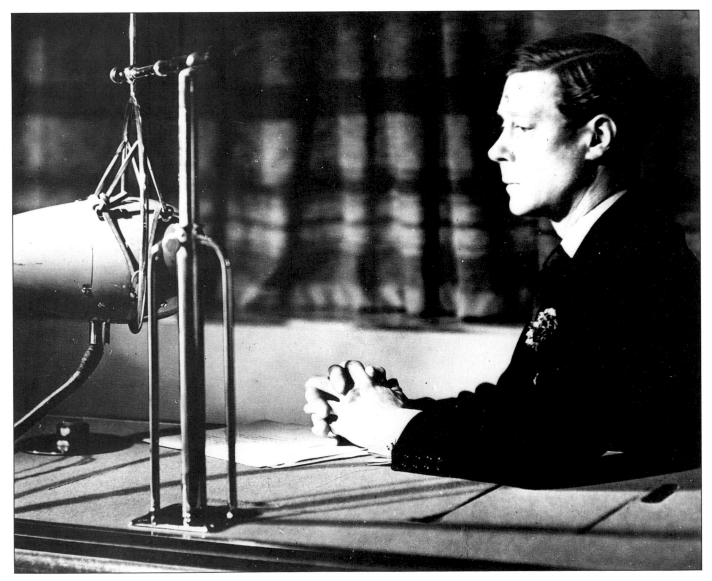

Above: In 1935 George V celebrated the 25th anniversary of his accession to the throne. The Silver Jubilee celebrations were splendid and included an appearance by almost the entire royal family on the balcony of the palace. From left to right, they include the Duke of York (later George VI); the Princess Royal (George V's only daughter, who was married to the Earl of Harewood); George V; Princess Margaret; Princess Elizabeth (the present Queen); Queen Mary; the Duchess of Kent; the Duke of Kent (George V's youngest son); and the Duchess of York, now the Queen Mother.

A year of turbulence for the royal family followed George V's death in January 1936. The new King, Edward VIII (far left), was in love with an American divorcée, Mrs Wallis Simpson, and eventually decided that he would renounce the throne in order to marry her. The photograph of the King on the right shows him with Mrs Simpson on holiday in Yugoslavia during the summer of 1936. His abdication in December brought his eldest brother, the Duke of York, to the throne as George VI. Edward VIII, by then the Duke of Windsor, left the country to live in France, with few regrets for his past life.

Garden Parties

Among the aspects of social life at Buckingham Palace which have continued without break from Victorian times to the present day are the garden parties held every July. Originally rather formal social occasions for a small part of upper-class society, the invitation list has in recent years been broadened to allow a wider cross-section of the population to attend. Some 8,000 guests are asked to each, so the chance of actually meeting the Queen are slim. However, she talks to as many people as possible on her stroll from the palace to the tea tents on the lawns, which are shown on the right in a 1924 photograph. The photograph on the left shows a garden party, also from the 1920s.

The guests for a garden party on the right are wearing the prescribed outfits: a long summer dress for the women and morning wear for the men. This stream of cars, left, waiting to enter the palace, was photographed in 1926: even today, garden parties still regularly cause traffic jams in the Mall.

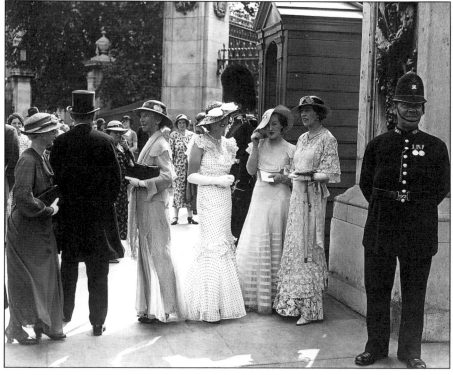

GEORGE VI

Below: The crisis of Edward VIII's abdication was followed by a period in which the royal family sought to emphasize the stability of the monarchy. This was greatly helped by the evident happiness of the new King's family life and the warm personality of his popular wife.

Left: Note the delightful contrast between this formal coronation photograph of 1937 left, showing the new King and Queen with their daughters, the Princesses Elizabeth and Margaret, and their more relaxed private life, as shown in the other photographs on these pages.

**Above: One of a series of informal
and relaxed photographs of George
VI and Queen Elizabeth taken at
Buckingham Palace. Corgis were the
royal family's favorite pet, as they
remain to the present day.**

Left: Queen Elizabeth at the piano in the White Drawing Room at Buckingham Palace, with George VI. The piano, by Sebastian and Pierre Erard, has a gilded and painted case; it was bought by Queen Victoria in 1856.

Left: The photograph of Queen Elizabeth with Princesses Elizabeth and Margaret was taken shortly after they had moved into Buckingham Palace in 1937. The children are playing the modern Broadwood piano which stands in the semi-circular bow window of the Music Room.

Right: These informal family portraits were taken at Buckingham Palace by Dorothy Wilding in 1946, 10 years after George VI's accession. Princess Elizabeth was then 20 and Princess Margaret, already a great beauty, was 16.

The new King and Queen were eager
to distance themselves from the
rather brittle glamor of Edward
VIII's court, which had regarded
them as somewhat dowdy. Queen
Elizabeth's decision to be
photographed by the young Cecil
Beaton was inspired: his pictures,
taken at Buckingham Palace in the
summer of 1939, created a new image
of fairytale romance.

Below and left: The Queen photographed by Beaton in the Palace's Blue Drawing Room. She originally wore a richly encrusted crinoline of gold and silver, but then changed into spangled white tulle. Beaton described her as "a fairy doll".

Right: The Queen photographed smiling under her parasol. She was amused that Beaton always photographed her directly against the sun; "we always have to spend our time running round to face the sun for the King's snapshots," she reportedly said.

Above left: During the war the state rooms of the palace were put to a variety of uses: this photograph shows "The Queen's Working Party". Consisting of members of the household staff at Buckingham Palace and the wives of employees of the Royal Mews, it met twice a week in the Blue Drawing Room to make clothes and surgical dressings for the Red Cross.

Below left: The King, inspecting the damage to the Palace with Queen Elizabeth, recorded in his diary how he and the Queen "were both upstairs . . . talking in my little sitting room overlooking the quadrangle. All of a sudden we heard an aircraft making a zooming noise above us, saw 2 bombs falling past the opposite side of the Palace and then heard 2 resounding crashes as the bombs fell in the quadrangle about 30 yds away . . ."

Below: Fortunately, nobody was hurt in the bomb raid on Buckingham Palace, and considering the number of bombs that had been dropped, the damage was not great. The worst casualty, the chapel, was never reinstated and after the war the shell was converted into a gallery where temporary public exhibitions of works from the Royal Collection are mounted.

Above left: Despite the war, Buckingham Palace continued to be used for some ceremonial occasions, such as investitures. This rare photograph of such an occasion was taken in the ballroom at the palace in March 1945 and shows the King decorating members of the royal services. Here he is presenting the CGM to Flight Sergeant Edward Durrans of Bomber Command.

Above: On August 15, 1945, VJ (Victory over Japan) Day was marked by more celebrations and the appearance of the royal family on the balcony of Buckingham Palace.

Left: The royal family won great admiration for their decision to stay in London during the Blitz, where they paid several morale-boosting visits to the East End, which had seen the worst of the bombing. This photograph shows the King and Queen on a return visit to Bethnal Green in East London on the day following VE (Victory in Europe) Day, May 8, 1945.

Left and below: 1948 was the year in which the King's health began to give cause for concern. In 1951 he had an operation for cancer of the lung and a year later he died. These photographs show the crowds gathering outside Buckingham Palace on February 6, 1952, waiting to read the formal announcement of his death, which had occurred earlier that morning at Sandringham.

Right: Cecil Beaton took some new photographs of Queen Elizabeth in 1948, when he experimented with an image very different from the fairytale romance of his 1939 photographs. He posed the Queen to suggest Victorian royal portraits by F. X. Winterhalter: she wears a specially made black Victorian crinoline designed by Norman Hartnell together with the "Indian" tiara, two diamond necklaces and a diamond brooch.

ELIZABETH II – THE EARLY YEARS

Right: Queen Elizabeth II was crowned on June 2, 1953, in an event which inspired enormous public enthusiasm, in part because for the first time it was watched by a large number of people through the new medium of television. The official Coronation photographs were taken by Cecil Beaton: here the Queen is shown in full regalia against a photographic backdrop of Westminster Abbey.

Below: Despite the rainy weather, immense crowds gathered outside Buckingham Palace to see the procession to Westminster Abbey.

Above: The Queen and her Maids of
Honour, photographed in
Buckingham Palace by Cecil Beaton.

Right: On July 10, 1947, it was formally announced from Buckingham Palace that the 21-year-old princess Elizabeth was engaged to be married to Lieutenant Philip Mountbatten of the Royal Navy, who, as the son of Prince and Princess Andrew of Greece, was a distant cousin. This photograph was taken after the announcement, and shows the Princess wearing her engagement ring in public for the first time. Their wedding, celebrated at Westminster Abbey on November 20, 1947, was the first great royal event of the post-war years, and provided an interval of cheer in a period of austerity. The formal wedding photographs (far right) of Princess Elizabeth and her new husband, created Duke of Edinburgh on the day of the marriage, were taken at Buckingham Palace.

Right: The wedding was followed by the traditional appearance of the royal family on the palace balcony. "Do remember", wrote George VI to his eldest daughter shortly after the wedding, "that your old home is still yours and do come back as often as possible. I can see that you are sublimely happy with Philip which is right, but don't forget us is the wish of your ever-loving and devoted Papa."

Left: Princess Elizabeth's first child, christened Charles Philip Arthur George, was born on November 14, 1948. Later that year, Cecil Beaton returned to Buckingham Palace to take the first official photographs of the new baby with his mother.

Below: The Princess's second child, Anne, was born on August 15, 1950. The two young children were photographed with their grandparents, the King and Queen, on Prince Charles's third birthday in 1951. These were the first photographs of the King to be published after his recent operation for cancer.

**Above: An affectionate moment
between the Queen and Princess
Anne, captured by Cecil Beaton.**

Above: In November 1972 the Queen and Prince Philip celebrated their silver wedding anniversary. To mark the occasion a group portrait of the royal family and their Kent cousins was taken at Buckingham Palace: surrounding the Queen (back row, left to right): Lord Snowdon; the Duke and Duchess of York, with Lord Nicholas Windsor on his mother's lap; Prince Michael of Kent; Prince Philip; the young Earl of St Andrews, eldest son of the Duke and Duchess of Kent; Prince Charles; Prince Andrew; Angus Ogilvy. Middle row: Princess Margaret; Queen Elizabeth, the Queen Mother; Princess Anne; and Princess Alexandra, flanked by her two children, Marina and James Ogilvy. The four children seated on the floor are (left to right) Lady Sarah Armstrong-Jones and Viscount Linley, Prince Edward and Lady Helen Windsor.

Left: The 1970s saw some of the happiest events celebrated by the royal family in recent years: on November 14, 1973 Princess Anne married a young cavalry officer, Captain Mark Phillips.

Right: With the Queen are Princess Anne, Earl Mountbatten of Burma (who was assassinated only two years later); Captain Mark Phillips (behind the Queen), Prince Philip, Princess Margaret and Prince Andrew.

Right: Perhaps the highpoint of Elizabeth II's reign so far has been the celebration in 1977 of the Silver Jubilee of her accession. The event aroused far more widespread enthusiasm than the Queen had expected: this photograph shows jubilant crowds clambering on the railings beside the Mall to get a better view of the royal family waving to them from the balcony.

Ceremonial Occasions

Left: Every year the Queen's official birthday in June is marked by the ceremony of Trooping the Colour on Horseguards Parade, at which the Queen takes the salue of the regiment whose color is being trooped. For many years she rode to and from Horseguards – this photograph shows her taking the salute, with Prince Philip on the left.

Below: "They're changing the guard at Buckingham Palace, Christopher Robin went down with Alice . . ." A. A. Milne's famous poem celebrates one of the best loved ceremonies in London: the daily changing of the guard, accompanied by lively music from regimental bands. The people watching the event were photographed in the 1960s; this was before the days of international tourism, which has resulted in enormous crowds gathering outside the palace, especially in summer.

Above: The young children peering through the palace railings are lucky to get such a close-up view!

Right: The Trooping of the Colour as it is performed today – the Queen no longer sits astride a horse but attends the ceremony in a carriage.

ELIZABETH II – RECENT TIMES

Right: The Queen as she appears today – the British monarchy is still envied throughout the world and she makes a dignified and respected figurehead.

Below: In 1980 Buckingham Palace was the backdrop for the celebrations for the 80th birthday of Queen Elizabeth, the Queen Mother. She is as old as this century!

Right: The Queen Mother appearing on the balcony at Buckingham Palace, flanked by her two daughters, the Queen and Princess Margaret. The crowd in the Mall which turned up to celebrate her birthday was enormous – after all, the Queen Mother is "Britain's best-loved Granny"!

Right: Away from the official photos we see the Queen and Queen Mother petting their favorite corgis – although the Queen does have a rather apprehensive expression on her face; her corgis do have a reputation for being extremely bad-tempered.

57

Presidents at the palace: Buckingham Palace makes a splendid backdrop for visits by foreign heads of state. In the last 30 years the Queen has entertained US presidents at Buckingham Palace on several occasions, some to formal banquets like that enjoyed by John and Jacqueline Kennedy (left) and Jimmy Carter (right), others to more relaxed lunches, such as that for Richard Nixon, on his first foreign tour in 1969 (below, with the Queen, Princess Anne and Prince Charles). In his autobiography, Ronald Reagan (below right, with Nancy Reagan and the Queen) describes a dinner held in his honor at the palace in 1982, at which – on the Queen Mother's prompting – he recited by heart the poem "The Shooting of Dan McGrew", much to the Queen's amusement.

Left: No royal event of recent years has thrilled the popular imagination to quite the extent as the marriage of the Prince of Wales to Lady Diana Spencer on July 29, 1981. This photograph captures for the first time at such an event, the bustle and excitement inside the palace. As the bridal party walk through the palace's picture gallery, the new Princess of Wales stops to encourage one of her younger bridesmaids as the Queen looks on.

Below left: Lady Di, as she was known to the world, takes a wave on the balcony together with Prince Charles and page Edward van Cutsem, as the new Princess of Wales. It didn't take long for the world's press to alter her title to Princess Di!

Above: A post-wedding photograph by Patrick Lichfield of (from left to right, top row) Princes Andrew and Edward, The Princess and Prince of Wales. Arrayed before them are the page boy and bridesmaids.

Below: The day of the wedding was blazing hot and people turned out in their thousands to cheer the royal couple. The rest watched their TVs at home – the day had been declared a national holiday in the U.K.

Above: The Prince and Princess of Wales are accompanied by Prince Edward and Prince Andrew, who shared the role of best man, and the pages and bridesmaids, led by Lady Sarah Armstrong-Jones.

Right: A brief moment away from formal poses for the Prince and Princess of Wales. Five years later, on July 23, 1986, Prince Andrew, created Duke of York on the day, was married to Sarah Ferguson, daughter of Major Ronald Ferguson, the Prince of Wales's polo manager. The couple wave to the crowds from the balcony (below) after the ceremony at Westminster Abbey.

Above: The view from St James's
Park of the west front of
Buckingham Palace as it appeared in
the 19th century. Over this past
century the view has hardy changed
at all.